How To Get Rich Without Winning The Lottery

Simple Methods to Get Rich, Retire Wealthy, and Have the Time of Your Life

By Keith Schreiter

KAAS Publishing
P.O. Box 890084
Houston, TX 77289
(281) 280-9800

www.FortuneNow.com

Printed in the United States of America

ISBN 1-892366-06-01

Cover design by: Kathie Sandlin

Table Of Contents

Disclaimer

In order to keep this book simple, I'm avoiding the discussions about inflation, taxes, investment risks, etc. I'm not an expert in any of these areas and I don't offer advice in these areas.

Once you've started earning and saving more money, you should seek the advice of professionals. After all, you can afford them when you have more money.

For those readers concerned about inflation or taxes in the examples I give, you can always add a year or two to the plans, earn a few more dollars, or adjust any of the ideas to meet your concerns.

All investments carry risk. Mutual funds and stocks go up and down. Real estate markets have good years and bad years. But having no savings and no investments guarantees failure.

How much money does it take to retire? For some people $250,000 will do just fine. For others, maybe $500,000 or $1,000,000 will make them feel rich. At some point, you'll find a certain amount of money will make you feel rich.

All names mentioned in this book are fictitious. They are a composite of many people I know who have learned that it's easy to be wealthy . . . when you know the rules.

Can you really be rich, retire wealthy and have the time of your life?

Yes!

And it doesn't matter if you are a rocket scientist, a taxi driver, a fisherman, a bank teller or even a backpacking bungy jumper. Anyone can be rich, retire wealthy, and have the time of his life by using some common sense ideas.

Wouldn't it be nice to have all the money you want? What would you buy?

A new or larger home?

A fancy sports car or luxury sedan?

College for the children?

A home for handicapped children?

A trip around the world?

Wouldn't it be nice to never have to work again? How would you spend your unlimited free time?

Would you play golf on the famous courses of the world?

Would you go to Hawaii?

Would you sail the Caribbean?

Would you take a year off to travel with your family?

Would you become an artist?

Not only is it possible to do all of these things – but **you can do them!**

You don't need any special talent or special privileges. Anyone can arrange his life so that he can accumulate wealth, have fun, or retire years before he is too old to enjoy it.

All you have to do is start by reading this book.

You'll learn that there are **several ways** to accumulate financial wealth. And you can choose to use any of the methods. There isn't just one unique method to financial wealth. There are several roads. You don't have to pick the same road your neighbor does. You choose the road that seems right for you.

The good news is that all these roads lead to financial wealth. You can achieve your financial goal no matter which course you take. So make sure to pick an enjoyable one so that you'll enjoy the journey.

Finally, remember that financial wealth does not equal success. It's only one part of life.

There are many important areas of life that have nothing to do with money. And, money isn't everything. What would this world be like if people didn't volunteer their time to help humanity? Would you want to live in a world without charity, love, or a willingness to help others? I don't think so.

However, this book is not about having a successful family life or spiritual life. We're going to talk about money.

Sit back, read and enjoy. This could be the most important book you'll ever read. It could be the book that changes your financial life.

If he can do it . . . so can you.

```
Name: John
Age: 23
Occupation: Taxi driver
Income: $29,000 a year
Retires wealthy: Age 43
```

At age 23, John was broke.

At age 43, John stopped driving his cab . . . and retired wealthy!

What happened?

Did John win the lottery? Did a rich aunt leave a large inheritance? Did he find buried treasure?

No.

Becoming wealthy and retired wasn't luck. John had a plan.

Just a small, simple change in John's work habits turned him from a cab driver into a full-time, wealthy retiree — a full 22 years before the "normal" retirement age of 65!

John will be playing a lot of golf.

We've all heard that knowledge is power. Well, John learned that **saving just a small amount of money each day** would change his life. The money he saved would grow and grow through the magic of compound interest.

Is this the only way to become wealthy?

No. It's just **one method** — the method John chose.

I'm going to share many **different** ways to wealth in this book. You can pick and choose which method is for you.

Back to John.

John has read that if you could save 10% of your salary and invest it wisely, you would accumulate wealth through the magic of compound interest.

Only one problem.

John couldn't save 10% of his salary. Between him and his family, they used 100% of his taxi driving earnings of $29,000 a year. There wasn't a penny left over for savings.

So John did the next best thing.

He decided to earn more money so he could build his savings nest egg. From now on he would make sure to work a bit longer each day until he had earned an extra $20 in fares. Some days he would get a $20 fare by working just 30 minutes longer. Other days he would have to work an extra hour or two.

But every day, five days a week, John earned his extra $20 to put into his savings.

As his savings grew, John invested in mutual funds. The average yearly return from his fund was about 10%. This is what happened.

At $20 a day, five days a week, John accumulated $100 a week in savings. That's $5,200 extra per year. Can you get rich saving $5,200 a year? Let's see what happens when you invest that money at 10% return.

Year	Amount Saved	Total Savings & Interest
1	5,200	5,200.00
2	5,200	10,920.00
3	5,200	17,212.00
4	5,200	24,133.20
5	5,200	31,746.52
6	5,200	40,121.17
7	5,200	49,333.29
8	5,200	59,466.62
9	5,200	70,613.28
10	5,200	82,874.61
11	5,200	96,362.07
12	5,200	111,198.28
13	5,200	127,518.10
14	5,200	145,469.91
15	5,200	165,216.90
16	5,200	186,938.60
17	5,200	210,832.45
18	5,200	237,115.70
19	5,200	266,027.27
20	5,200	297,830.00

At the end of just 20 years, John's $100 a week contributions have grown to $297,830!

At 10% interest, that's $29,783 a year for John and his family — slightly more than John's original yearly earnings.

Now with his new $29,783 income from his investments, John never has to work again if he chooses. He just joined the ranks of the rich and retired.

What about the future?

John says, "In another 22 years I'll be eligible for Social Security retirement benefits. That will be just like a pay raise. Meanwhile, I plan to enjoy life 24 hours a day, seven days a week!

Why some people
will never be wealthy.

I have a good friend who won't become wealthy. He says he'd like more money in his life, but here is how our conversations go:

> **Me:** "You know that if you invested in real estate you would have paid off properties in ten or twenty years. Then you could quit that job you hate and go fishing."

> **Friend:** "No way do I want to own a rental house or a couple of apartments. I don't want to deal with tenants, repairs, or collecting rent. That's not for me."

> **Me:** "Did you ever think about getting a part-time job? You could invest the extra income in some mutual funds and let them accumulate. After awhile, your stocks could give you enough dividends so you wouldn't need to commute to that job every morning."

> **Friend:** "No way could I work a part-time job. I need time to relax and enjoy that new big screen television I bought for the kids. Plus, I'm so burned out at the end of the day from my regular job that I can barely make it to my recliner.

> "And part-time jobs don't pay as much as my full-time job. Why should I work for less? And

the stock market might go down and I'd lose money. Plus I can't wait years to retire. I want to retire right now."

Me: "Did you ever think of going to night school? You could get the training to get a big advancement and pay raise in your regular job. Then you'd have extra money to invest to start creating your wealth nest egg."

Friend: "Night school? Are you kidding? Once I finished high school I told myself I'd never have to study or learn again. I can't stand classrooms."

Me: "Why not start a small part-time business? You could gradually grow the business to become a full-time profession or at least you could take the part-time earnings and invest them for your retirement. Ever think about that?"

Friend: "No. That's too risky. What if I couldn't get any customers or someone didn't pay me? Then I'd have to work for nothing just to get it started. I want to be paid for every hour I work. I deserve it. Plus, I don't want to be tied down to a lease or employee problems. That's all too much stress and bother."

And so the conversation goes.

No matter what is suggested, my friend has a reason why it won't work for him. Nothing will work for this kind of person – not even a business where all you have to do is watch cable television all day. This type of person would say that all that television watching would be too hard on the eyes.

This type of excuse-driven person will never be wealthy. Sure, he might say he wants to be wealthy, but only if becoming wealthy was a worry-free, guaranteed proposition that required no work, no effort, no risk, no input or no investment on his part.

Good luck finding that kind of deal in today's world.

This book is **not** for my friend, or people like my friend.

This book is for doers – people who want to become wealthy and are willing to do something about it.

If you love automobiles, you can still be wealthy.

```
Name: Harry
Age: 31
Occupation: Carpenter
Income: $25,000 a year
Retires wealthy: Age 41
```

Harry loves cars. He dreams about cars. He details cars. And he loves to go to car shows.

His hobby and passion is to purchase used cars, do minor repairs, clean and detail the car, and then resell the car for an $800 profit. It's nice to make a profit on your hobby!

So what is Harry's goal for his part-time hobby/business? He wants to resell two cars a month, ten months out of the year. The other two months are reserved for ski trips. That's a total of 20 cars sold a year at $800 profit each — for a grand total of $16,000 of extra yearly income.

What does Harry do with his extra money?

He invests it wisely in stocks, his own house, and re-invests in his hobby/business by purchasing more expensive cars that can give him higher profits.

If Harry averages a 10% return on his nest-egg fund (actually, he earns much more because he makes tremendous profits when he reinvests in cars), here is what would happen in just 10 years:

Year	Amount Saved	Total Savings & Interest
1	16,000	16,000
2	16,000	33,600
3	16,000	52,960
4	16,000	74,256
5	16,000	97,681.60
6	16,000	123,449.76
7	16,000	151,794.74
8	16,000	182,974.21
9	16,000	217,271.63
10	16,000	254,998.79

So in just 10 years, Harry's fund has over $250,000. At a 10% return, Harry can just sit back and collect $25,000 a year.

Harry says, "I figure I can ski six months a year in Colorado and six months a year in New Zealand."

And, if Harry ever needs a few extra dollars, he can always fix up a car or two during the year.

A one-minute pep talk.

Let's look at why some people become rich while other people just talk about it.

Most people who have attained financial freedom and wealth did it on their own. It wasn't given to them. They didn't have lucky breaks.

They made it happen.

There is the old saying:

> Some people make things happen.
> Some people watch things happen.
> Other people just sit and wonder,
> "What's happening?"

Because you are reading this book, I'm sure that you are in the first group of people, those people who make things happen.

This book will show you some **simple**, **consistent small actions**. Anybody can do these simple actions — if they choose. What happens when you do these actions? Every month your bank account will grow larger and larger until one day you'll declare, "I'm rich!"

You'll learn that becoming rich is not a single, spectacular event. Instead, you'll learn how to accumulate wealth from a series of **small actions** that anyone can do.

As you read this book, remember that your mind is like a parachute – it works better when it is open.

So open up your mind and observe how these small actions will change your financial life.

Your reward for investing 90 minutes in this book?

When you finish this book you'll have your personal step-by-step formula for your MBA (Massive Bank Account).

So how much money do you need to be wealthy?

What does financial wealth mean to you?

- Having a million dollars in your savings account?
- Receiving a check in your mailbox every month that covers your monthly expenses?
- Never having to go to work again?

These are just some of the definitions of financial wealth. Your definition might be quite different from anyone else's. However, no matter how you describe financial wealth – you can get there using one of the many proven paths mentioned in this book.

Let's imagine that financial wealth means that you have enough money to live the lifestyle you want – and you never have to go to work again. Fair enough?

In other words, you have all the money you need to lead a comfortable life. How much is that? Let's look at some examples.

1. Ed loves to camp out in "fishing territory." All Ed needs is $500 a month for a few expenses as his tent is already paid for and he plans to eat the fish he catches.

2. Monica needs $1,500 a month to pay her day-to-day expenses while she writes novels.

3. Alex needs $6,000 a month to travel the world and explore.

4. Rita needs $10,000 a month for her lifestyle and charities.

As you see, financial independence means something different for everyone. Only you can decide what's right for you.

So how do you get that money you need to be financially free?

I'm going to show you several ways to get that money, and at least one of those ways will work for you.

But first, I have to discuss something very important concerning your job.

Your job won't make you wealthy. You'll never earn enough.

This is a big error that most people make. They believe that their job can make them wealthy.

Look around you. How many wealthy job holders do you see in your neighborhood?

Jobs are good. They pay the rent or mortgage. They buy our clothes and food. However, you do have to go to work to get paid. This is a major inconvenience.

If you have to go to work every day to get paid, you're not financially free. You have to continue to work for a living. And chances are that your job doesn't pay you enough to lead the style of life you want.

For instance, let's say that you want five weeks vacation this summer with the family. The job gives you two weeks vacation. You're not wealthy if you don't have the freedom to take those additional weeks of vacation with the family.

Another problem is that jobs just don't pay enough to be financially free. Think about your present job. Does it pay enough? Can you do almost anything you want on your present salary? Probably not.

And no matter how hard you work, no matter how many extra hours you work, you are still limited to what you can earn. You are only one person. You only have 24 hours in a day.

Okay. So a job has limits. A job won't make us wealthy. Then where do we go to become wealthy? How else can we have a regular monthly check arrive in our mailbox that pays for the lifestyle we want?

Famous shortcuts to wealth.
Can these work for you?

There are lots of ways to become wealthy. Here are just a few.

Inherit wealth.

I like this one. No work, no sweat, no worries.

The problem is that it's hard to get adopted by rich and sickly parents. There aren't many of these people around. While this method works, it only works for a few. If you were one of the lucky few, well, you wouldn't be reading this book. You'd be cruising the Caribbean.

Marry someone who is already incredibly rich.

If you're not married now, hey, there is still time for you to find a wealthy spouse. But that's not the subject of this book as again, this is a way to wealth that few can do.

Hit it big in the stock market.

Your shares double and triple in price. However, there is a problem. You have to already be rich to buy lots of stock. Yes, there's always a catch.

Win the lottery.

Math experts already know the truth:

> The lottery is a voluntary tax on
> people who are really bad at math.

You are about 100 times more likely to be struck by lightning than to win the lottery. To put that into perspective, the odds are that you'd be struck by lightning 100 times before winning the lottery. And after being zapped by lightning 100 times, do you really think you'd feel like going out and having a good time spending your lottery winnings?

Lottery is entertainment – a reason to watch television to check if your number won a dollar or two. Play the lottery for fun. Don't use it for your primary investment vehicle.

Write a hit song. Or sing a hit song.

I can't sing. In fact, I can barely hum. If you are one of those rare individuals with superstar musical talent – go for it! Use that talent. Make a million or two and enjoy. However, this book isn't about writing hit songs. So if you're like me and can't hold a tune, relax. There are plenty of other ways to financial independence.

How about writing that great romance novel?

Well, that's a way to financial wealth, but a very rare way. Very few people are able to take this path. This book is for the rest of us.

Well, if these well-known ways to wealth won't work for most of us, then how do average people become wealthy?

Change people's buying habits
for an extra $25,000 a year.

```
Name: Kathleen
Age: 24
Occupation: Bank teller
Income: $25,000 a year
Retires wealthy: Age 26
```

Kathleen didn't want to wait years and years for what she wanted to do in life: compose and perform her music.

To really achieve her musical goals, Kathleen would need to travel, study, and practice in such places as New Orleans, New York City, London, Paris and Australia. There would be no time for a regular or part-time job. Her quest would be a total immersion into the world of music.

Kathleen decided to start a part-time network marketing career. *She would simply change people's buying habits.* Instead of purchasing certain items at the local store, they would now purchase them through Kathleen's catalog.

At first, the commissions and bonuses were barely $100 a month. As each month passed, word-of-mouth advertising drew more and more people to change their purchasing habits. At the end of one year, Kathleen was earning an extra $250 a month.

And then it really began to grow.

At the end of two years, Kathleen's bonus check exceeded $2,000 a month and continued to grow. Now she was making as much money from her part-time network marketing career as she was from her full-time job.

Kathleen's decision?

Quit the bank teller job.

Now she could study, research, compose and perform music full-time while her monthly network marketing bonus check paid the bills.

How average people accumulate above-average wealth.

It's not rocket science. Millions of ordinary people have become millionaires through their own initiative — with no help from wealthy family members or lucky lottery numbers.

A job is one way to earn money but, as I mentioned earlier, a job has limits.

You can only earn so much per hour. You can only work so many hours in a day. You can't really be wealthy if you have to be at work all day.

So, we need another source of income to replace our job income if we're going to be wealthy. There are two easy sources for more money in our lives:

#1: We can have our money working for us.

When our money is in a bank savings account, in investment real estate, or in mutual funds, our money is working for us 24 hours a day, even while we're sleeping. If we have enough money invested, our monthly interest and dividends can match or exceed our normal job income. That means that we can retire from our job and do what we want.

Sounds great, but what's the catch?

Most of us will ask:

"Where will I get all this money to put into investments?"

It's not that hard. I'll show you how in the next couple of chapters. You can easily accumulate an investment nest egg from:

- ◆ A part-time job

- ◆ A part-time business

- ◆ Saving a little bit out of every paycheck

- ◆ Having your income tax preparer arrange your finances so that you pay less in taxes.

- ◆ Reducing your personal expenses.

Now, all these methods look small but, believe me, over time they can help you accumulate all the investment money you need to retire wealthy.

This is great news! This means that most people can become wealthy by making only a slight change in their present life. Before I show you how this will work, there is yet another source of more money in our lives.

#2: We can have other people working for us.

Think about the owner of the company you work for. I bet this person makes more money than any of the employees. If the owner earns five times more money than the average employee does, I don't think the owner works five times more hours, do you?

The business owner has only 24 hours in a day just like you and me. However, business owners understand the magic word: leverage. They leverage their time and efforts through other people. They earn a little bit from every employee's efforts. And those little bits really add up.

So you're thinking, "I'm not ready to be a business owner. I don't know enough about business or the risks."

Don't worry. You don't have to own a business with lots of employees and equipment to use the principle of leverage. I'll show you how to use leverage later on in this book. But for now, all you have to remember is that you can leverage your time and income through other people.

Do you have to have a business?

No. It's just another way to financial wealth. Remember what I said at the beginning of this book? I said that there are many roads to financial wealth. You don't have to follow any particular road. I'll just point out several different roads and then it's up to you to choose your route.

To summarize, there are three ways you can have money coming to you each month:

1. **Work a job – get a check.**

2. **Have your money work for you.**

3. **Have other people work for you.**

Almost everyone has mastered how to get a job and get a check. But that's not what we want.

We want time freedom to do what we want and to have enough money to do what we want. A job won't get us there.

So, we must either have our money work for us, or have other people work for us.

Now let's get on with accumulating some wealth. Let's talk about some ways to get our money working for us.

Money to invest? What money?

If you're going to have money working for you, the first thing to do is to get some money, right?

I know what you are probably thinking,

> "Sure I understand that it takes money to make money, but I don't have any money. I can't pay my bills now. I want more money, but I can't save any money on my present income. I'd like to use this method, but where will I get the money?"

Let's talk about method #1 for getting some money to start your investments. Remember, you want money working for you so you don't have to do all the work.

If you don't want to use method #1, that's okay. It's only one of the methods that are available for your use. But you might want to give this method a try since the discipline it teaches is a discipline you'll need to create permanent wealth. So here it is, method #1:

Save a little bit of money out of each paycheck.

That's it? That's one of the secret methods to becoming wealthy?

Yes. Pretty simple, isn't it? Regular savings and compound interest mean financial wealth to those disciplined individuals who have patience.

But you can't save any money out of your paycheck? Your bills are too high?

I bet anyone could save an extra $100 a month out of his paycheck and still pay his bills. How?

Just pretend that your boss gave you a $100 cut in pay. If you received a $100 cut in pay, would that be the end of the world? Would you and your family starve? Would Western Civilization come to an end?

I don't think so. When things get a bit harder, we simply adjust. I bet some time in your life that you made an income that was at least $100 a month less than what you are making now. You were able to survive then, right?

So pretend you just got a $100 cut in pay. What would you do? Maybe you would:

- Discontinue cable television.
- Eat out at restaurants less frequently.
- Stop buying new clothing every fashion season.
- Go to fewer movies.
- Carry your lunch to work.
- Stop smoking or drinking designer beer.
- Make fewer long distance telephone calls.
- Have only one telephone line in your home instead of two.
- Spend your vacation at your in-laws' house instead of that condo on the beach.
- Trade in your car for a less expensive model.

But you say:

"Oh no, I couldn't do any of these things!"

Then I would say that all of those things are more important to you than becoming wealthy. For instance, if you keep your cable television because you enjoy the extra channels, you might be saying to yourself, "I want the pleasure of watching cable television channels more than I want to be wealthy." If that's what you want, that's okay. Just realize that you are making the choice and <u>this particular method may not work for you.</u>

If you have a brand new car with a high car payment – well, you may realize that who you are does not depend on the model of your car.

A three-year-old car will get you to work just fine. If your friends think it's necessary to spend lots of money on a depreciating asset like a car, well, maybe they need to read this book if they ever intend to be wealthy.

What if you had to move to a smaller apartment to become wealthy? If you moved from an expensive three-bedroom waterfront apartment to a less plush two-bedroom apartment, you could literally save hundreds of dollars a month. Maybe you could save enough to qualify to purchase your first home.

But don't cut your budget on the really important things in life.

Have some balance in your life. Don't be like my friend, Tom, who said,

> "I give my wife flowers every year for our anniversary. Maybe I should invest that $65 in-

stead into my investment fund? That will certainly help it grow."

Well, the investment fund will grow slightly faster, but Tom will only get half of the fund. That's not smart thinking.

So who determines if I'll be wealthy?

The choice to be wealthy is yours. It's totally up to you if you want extra money every month that can go to work for you.

Wealthy individuals accumulated money and became wealthy by following one basic truth:

Spend less than you earn – invest the difference.

You can achieve this by using the first method we've discussed. By simply lowering your expenses, you'll have extra money to invest every month.

If lowering your expenses is distasteful, how else can you arrange your finances so that you'll spend less than you earn?

Easy, just try method #2.

Method #2:

Earn more money every month.

If your expenses stay the same, you can have lots of extra money to invest if you simply increase your monthly income.

There are several ways of increasing your monthly income. Let's look at a few.

You could work overtime on your job.

Those extra hours can add up in a hurry. Let's say that you just work five extra hours a week. That's 20 extra hours a month. If your net pay is $10 an hour, you'll have an extra $200 to invest every month. It won't take long to build a sizable investment fund at this rate.

For example, if you put aside $200 a month at 10% interest for 30 years, you'd have a total of $394,785.65 in your investment fund. That's a lot of money!

Here is what just one forward-thinking woman is doing.

```
Name: Nancy
Age: 35
Occupation: Accounting Clerk
Income: $19,000 a year
Will start traveling the world: Age 43
```

Travel the world? That's Nancy's goal. And she doesn't want to wait 30 years before she starts. Here is her plan.

By working an average of nine hours a week overtime she earns an extra $100 a week. By investing it wisely, Nancy will have over $50,000 in her investment fund in just eight years. At 10% return, Nancy will collect an extra $5,000 a year in income. That's about one-fourth of her regular salary.

This means that Nancy can work nine months out of the year, and use the income from her investment fund for the remaining three months. This will be Nancy's travel time.

Imagine having a three-month vacation every year to travel wherever you like.

You could go to school, learn new skills and get a big promotion.

Caution: Big promotions cause many people to create big expenses. For instance, let's say that you presently earn $30,000 a year and you get that big promotion and a raise to $50,000 a year. Do you have an extra $20,000 a year to put in your investment fund?

Probably not. First, there are taxes. There would still be plenty of money left for a massive investment fund, but human nature causes many people to spend that extra money on:

- ♦ A new car
- ♦ A larger home
- ♦ Private school for the kids
- ♦ New suits
- ♦ That long-awaited vacation
- ♦ Country club membership
- ♦ That stereo entertainment center that covers the wall, etc.

See the problem? Promotions and raises in salary cause most people to spend more money. Don't fall into that trap. If you are age 30 and could invest $10,000 of that $20,000 raise each year, here is how much you'd have in your investment fund, assuming your fund earned a 10% return:

Duration	Total Savings & Interest
5 years (age 35)	61,051.00
10 years (age 40)	159,374.25
15 years (age 45)	317,724.82
20 years (age 50)	572,749.99
25 years (age 55)	983,470.59
30 years (age 60)	1,644,940.23
35 years (age 65)	2,710,243.68

I think I'll stop here at age 65. This would be more than enough money for most of us.

Get a part-time job.

Why not work a few extra hours a week to earn that extra investment money you need? The more money you invest, the harder your investment money can work for you.

There are plenty of part-time jobs and most of them are available to responsible, hard-working people. You can find an amazing variety of part-time work, such as:

- Telemarketing
- Pizza delivery
- Newspaper delivery
- Fast food cashier
- Alarm installer
- Information tracer
- Sales
- Bookkeeping
- Retail sales
- Inventory counter
- Janitorial
- Adult education teacher
- Consulting, etc.

```
Name: Herman
Age: 28
Occupation: Personnel Director
Income: $35,000 a year
Will retire wealthy: Age 38
```

Herman has a nice job. Suit and tie, nice office, pleasant working conditions. The only thing that irritates Herman is that he has to go to work. He hates commuting. He hates leaving his wife and small son every day.

Here is Herman's plan.

On Friday and Saturday nights, Herman delivers pizza in his suburban hometown. With an average net of $50 an evening, Herman has an extra $100 a week to put into his investment fund.

And because he is disciplined, that's what Herman has done over the past two years. Already his investment fund is over $11,000. That's more than the vice-president of his company has in his savings account. You see, it's not how much you earn that counts. **It's how much you save**.

Herman also plans to add his next pay raise to his investment fund. Between his part-time job of delivering pizzas and his additional deposits from his future pay raises, Herman plans to downsize himself to a three-day workweek by age 33 and to totally retire by age 38.

Why downsize to a three-day workweek? Because Herman loves soccer and wants to coach his son, and travel with him through his playing days at school.

And all this was possible from delivering a few pizzas!

Start a part-time business.

It's easier than you think. Most businesses today are service businesses, not manufacturing businesses. That means you won't have to invest a lot of money into equipment, buildings and employees.

In fact, most small businesses are one-person operations out of the home. That one person can be you.

If you know how to clean swimming pools, why not start a swimming pool cleaning service? At $30 per week per pool, you'd only need two customers to have an extra $240 a month. You can create a large investment fund with only a $240 a month contribution.

But what if you had ten customers? This means you'd have two pools to clean every weekday after work. Ten customers would mean an extra $1,200 a month for your investment fund! Now you're talking about taking the fast track to wealth.

If you'd invest $1,200 a month at 10% return, you'd have:

Duration	Total Savings & Interest
5 years	92,924.49
10 years	245,813.97
20 years	911,242.60
30 years	2,712,585.51

And all of this came from just cleaning two pools every weekday after work.

What other examples of part-time businesses can you do?

♦ Can you wash and detail cars?

♦ Can you help people prepare their taxes?

♦ Can you show people how to use their computer?

♦ Can you mow lawns?

♦ Can you start your own part-time delivery service?

♦ Can you sell products or services part-time?

♦ Can you write computer programs?

♦ Can you grow rare vegetables or herbs for resale?

♦ Can you cater food to large parties?

♦ Can you arrange and organize weddings?

♦ Can you be a wedding photographer on Saturdays?

♦ Can you do bookkeeping for small companies?

♦ Can you do home remodeling?

The possibilities are endless. There is something you can do, or something you can learn, so that you can start your own part-time business.

```
Name: Larry
Age: 38
Occupation: Fireman
Income: $31,000 a year
Will retire wealthy: Age 53
```

Larry lives in Canada and loves to fish. His fireman schedule is unusual. A couple of 24-hour shifts and then several days off. Great for some fun fishing trips in the summer, but what about the winter?

In winter, Larry runs a snow removal business alongside his job as a fireman. During the five months of snow, Larry nets about $300 a week after paying a part-time employee to help for those times when Larry is at work.

With a net income of over $6,000 a season, Larry's investment fund grows and grows. He chose starting a snow removal business so that it wouldn't interfere with his summer fishing trips.

Having a part-time business doesn't mean you have to give up your free time and hobbies. Simply pick the type of part-time business that fits your needs and lifestyle.

Here is what the extra $6,000 a year means to Larry. He started his plan about four years ago at age 34.

Duration	Total Savings & Interest
Present balance (age 38)	27,846.00
5 more years (age 43)	81,476.86
10 more years (age 53)	306,954.54

At 10% return, Larry can now retire full-time. The fish had better be scared. And what about Larry's fireman pension? Well, that will just be extra money he won't need.

Is a part-time business the answer for everyone?

No.

Many times a part-time business takes time to become profitable. Or, maybe you're happy with your job and just prefer to work overtime to get that extra investment money.

A part-time business is a great way to accumulate the extra investment money you need, but it's not the only way.

Remember, pick the road to financial wealth that's right for you.

So far we've covered four ways to get that extra investment money you need by:

1. **Reducing your monthly expenses.**

2. **Earning extra money by working overtime.**

3. **Finding a part-time job.**

4. **Starting your own part-time business.**

But these four methods aren't the only ways to become wealthy. Let's look at some more possibilities.

Own your own home.

At the very least, if you intend to be wealthy, you'll want to own your own home. Why?

There are two types of people.

1. **The people who rent for 25 years and collect a worthless pile of rent receipts.**

2. **The people who pay a mortgage for 25 years and end up with a $100,000 or $200,000 or $300,000 home.**

Both groups of people made a payment every month. The people who rent saw their monthly payments rise every year with inflation.

The homeowners were happy to have a fixed mortgage payment that seemed to get smaller every year as their income increased.

Having a $200,000 home completely paid for 25 years from now means you'll have $200,000 more in your investment fund. And as a side benefit, owning your own home means:

- ◆ You can paint it any color you want.

- ◆ You don't have to move because the landlord had a bad day.

- ◆ Every mortgage payment is building equity in your retirement fund.

Important point: More millionaires have been created through real estate than any other method. Owning your own home is the simplest, least demanding way of investing in real estate.

How Ann used her home to retire.

Name: Ann
Age: 26
Occupation: Accounting
Income: $30,000 a year
Retires wealthy: Age 47

This is a great example of having our money work for us.

Ann had a good job that paid the bills. She made mortgage payments and car payments just like everyone else on her block. <u>But, Ann knew a secret</u>.

Years ago when Ann applied for her mortgage, the loan officer reviewed her finances. The loan officer said:

> "Your mortgage payment can only be 33% of your income. If it's more than that, you might not be able to afford your home."

Nothing too earth-shattering here. Everyone needs some money left over for food, car payments, clothing, vacations, etc. However, this one statement got Ann thinking:

> "If my mortgage equals one-third of my income . . . then, what would happen if I owned three homes — and all were paid for?"

For example, Ann earns $2,500 a month and her mortgage payment is one-third of that, about $833 a month.

If Ann paid her mortgage faster by making larger payments, in a few years her mortgage would be paid off and she would own her home free and clear. No more mortgage payments!

Of course Ann would have to sacrifice a few dinners out, or get a small raise, or earn extra money from a part-time job, but by adding just $100 a month to her regular mortgage payment could mean reducing her 25-year mortgage to less than 19 years.

Or, by adding just $200 a month to her regular mortgage payment could mean reducing her 25-year mortgage ($108,000 mortgage @ 8% interest) to only a 15-year mortgage.

Or, by adding just $400 a month to her regular mortgage payment could mean reducing her 25-year mortgage to only an 11-year mortgage. This 11-year accelerated plan was Ann's choice.

Get the picture? Ann is going to get pay raises in her future, so it will get easier and easier to add a few extra dollars to pay off her mortgage.

But it gets better.

Once Ann no longer has a mortgage payment, what will she do with the extra $1,000 every month?

Here's one idea.

Ann buys the house next door. Maybe the mortgage, insurance and taxes on the house next door is $1,000 a month, but the renters pay $1,000 in rent so there is no extra money out of Ann's pocket. If Ann simply keeps the house next door for 25 years, the renters will pay off the mortgage.

That means that the rental income from the house next door will be free and clear extra money for Ann to spend.

However, Ann doesn't wait 25 years for the tenants to pay off the mortgage. She pays the bank $2,000 a month and pays off the mortgage in just over **six years**. Where did she get the $2,000?

She collected $1,000 from the tenants. Since Ann has already paid off the mortgage on her home, she adds that extra $1,000 she used to pay on her personal mortgage to help pay off the mortgage on the house next door.

Why did Ann purchase the house next door?

Because it didn't have to be a bargain.

Ann didn't want to be a full-time real estate super investor. She knew that if the house next door were reasonably priced, she would make money.

For example, if you buy a $100,000 home today, in 25 years it may well be worth $200,000 because of inflation. So does it really matter if you bought the home for $99,000 or for $101,000? Not really.

Once you have paid off the home, you're going to have a $200,000 asset. When you invest long-term, you don't have to worry about getting the lowest price on your transaction.

What happens in six years when Ann no longer has to make mortgage payments next door?

She buys the house on the other side of her home.

If the mortgage is $1,000, and the tenants pay $1,000 rent, and Ann adds the $1,000 rent from the previous home she bought, plus Ann adds $1,000 that she used to pay on her mortgage, wow!!!

Ann can make a $3,000 a month mortgage payment and pay off the next house in just four years.

Now, what does Ann have?

Financial freedom and retirement.

Here are her new finances.

Before, Ann needed $2,500 a month to take care of her living expenses and lifestyle.

But that $2,500 monthly overhead included $833 Ann paid on her mortgage. Since she no longer has mortgage payments, Ann only needs $1,667 a month for living expenses.

Where can Ann get that $1,667?

From collecting rent from the two houses that she owns free and clear of any mortgages. And there still is enough rent money left over for taxes, insurance, and minor repairs.

So if Ann decided never to go to work again, that's okay. She has all the money she needs to retire.

So if your mortgage is one-third of your income, all you need to do is to own three houses. One to live in, and two for income. If you could accomplish this, you'd be retired at your present lifestyle.

If you wanted a more opulent lifestyle, you would simply purchase another home.

If you were in a hurry to retire, you could use leverage to purchase all three homes at once. This means more debt and more risk, but many have done it.

In Ann's example, she used a minimum of debt. This made it easy to sleep at night. But even though she used this very, very conservative approach, she was still able to retire in less than 20 years.

So if you want to retire sooner with this method, use more leverage or add more money to your mortgage payments.

What about maintenance and repairs?

Well, with inflation, rents continue to go up. When was the last time you saw rents go down in your neighborhood? It doesn't happen very often, or for very long.

Ann can simply save the extra money from the increased rent to use for any maintenance and repairs.

Managing the rental house next door is easy because it's next door. This is a simple, easy way to invest in real estate.

Do you have to use Ann's method of real estate investing to build your financial wealth?

No. It's just one method.

However, isn't it nice when other people (tenants) help you retire faster?

How to leverage your time and income through other people.

The first way to increase your income and build your investment fund is to have **your** money work for you. And, as we have seen, there are several ways to accumulate the money you need to get your investment fund started.

The second way to build your investment fund fast is through the principle of leverage. Since you can only do so much yourself, use the leverage of other people's efforts to help you accumulate and build your investment fund faster.

Here's how to use people leverage in your business.

Remember that part-time pool cleaning business we talked about? The business where you could personally clean ten pools a week?

As the only employee of your business, you are limited to how many pools you can clean after you get off work, right? If you wanted to earn more money by increasing the number of pools you clean, then you'd have to hire a helper.

Maybe you decide to pay your helper $20 for every pool he cleans. Since you charge the homeowner $30 for every pool cleaning, you'd make an extra $10 whenever your helper cleaned a pool.

The more pools your helper cleans, the more money you make. This is what we mean by leveraging your time and effort through other people.

Do you have to hire more employees and use this leverage principle?

No. It's just another method to build your investment fund. Having extra options and choices are always nice.

Whenever you start a business you can use this people-leveraging principle to quickly build your investment fund. However, many people won't use this means of leveraging because:

- ♦ They don't want employee headaches.
- ♦ They want to keep their business small and manageable.
- ♦ They don't want to be responsible for overseeing other people.
- ♦ They don't want the paperwork and insurance headaches, etc.

If this method of people leveraging doesn't appeal to you, there is yet another way to leverage your efforts.

It's called network marketing.

Most people do network marketing every day, but they just don't get paid for it.

You see, network marketing is nothing more than **recommending** and **promoting** what you like. If

you're like most people, you recommend and pro-
mote:

- ◆ Sports teams
- ◆ Babysitters
- ◆ Brands of beer
- ◆ Pediatricians
- ◆ Places to shop for clothes
- ◆ Someone who mows your lawn
- ◆ Movies
- ◆ Restaurants
- ◆ Places to go on vacation
- ◆ Funny jokes you've heard
- ◆ Car mechanics, etc.

Since you recommend and promote daily, why not get paid for it, right?

Or, you can continue recommending and promoting for free. Free isn't bad. Charity work makes the
world a better place. But if you're tired of working
for free, and want to join some smart entrepreneurs
who get an extra income in their mailbox every
month, you'll want to check out network marketing.

Hundreds of companies will pay you commissions
and bonuses for what you do naturally every day,
recommending and promoting what you like.

These companies will actually pay you for recommending and promoting their goods or services. Instead of spending money on television advertising or

newspaper ads, these companies rely on word-of-mouth promotion.

Think about it. Which long distance service would you try?

1. The long distance service promoted on television by an actor you didn't like?

2. Or, the long distance service recommended by your mother or your best friend?

Or which multi-vitamin product would you try?

1. The multi-vitamin promoted on television by the mega-pharmaceutical conglomerate?

2. Or, the multi-vitamin product recommended by your classmate who now claims to feel ten years younger?

Thousands of different goods and services are promoted through network marketing. Word-of-mouth advertising is powerful. Traditional media doesn't stand a chance against a trusted friend's recommendation.

So how does the "people leverage" principle fit into network marketing?

Think of network marketing as a family tree or genealogy. Companies that use network marketing to distribute their goods and services not only pay you for telling other people, but also when the people you tell go out and tell other people, etc., etc., etc. In other words, you could tell A who tells B who tells C who tells D and so on, and you could earn a monthly bonus check on all of their usage and sales.

That's people leveraging at work.

Some people use their network marketing income to accelerate their investment fund. In some cases, their part-time network marketing income exceeded the income from their regular job so they decided to make network marketing their full-time profession.

Over five million people (that's a lot of people) are already collecting an extra income from their part-time network marketing business in the United States alone. Since you are already recommending and promoting what you like, shouldn't you consider getting paid for it too?

Here is why I like network marketing.

Network marketing is one of the fastest ways to a quick retirement.

This is important, especially if you're 45 or 50 years old and don't have a lot of time for your money to earn compound interest.

So if you're no longer young, don't panic. Network marketing can help you catch up on your investment fund in a hurry.

But you can also do network marketing when you're young.

At age 18 I graduated from high school and started working my network marketing business. I found two main benefits:

1. I earned several thousand dollars extra for my investment fund, and

2. The network marketing company had a program that paid for a new car. Since they were going to pay for the car of my choice, I chose a Pontiac Firebird. If they didn't have that car bonus program, I'm sure that I'd still be driving my 1990 Dodge Colt.

I lived with my parents until I was 23. This isn't easy when all your friends have their own apartments. However, this allowed me to save huge amounts of my paycheck from my regular graphics design job, plus I could also save all my income from my part-time network marketing business. Since I now earn over $60,000 a year from my part-time network marketing business, this really adds up.

Please note that my network marketing income was almost nothing during my first year. It has gradually, but consistently, increased over the six years.

At age 23 I finally purchased my own home. I felt that my investment fund was growing nicely, plus I could still handle the mortgage payment easily from the paycheck from my job.

By avoiding debt, by avoiding car payments, and by spending less than I earn, it's easy to live without the stress of worrying about which bills to pay first.

And since I avoid debt, my monthly overhead is quite low. This allows me to still spend money for vacations, travel and entertainment without guilt.

Do you have to do network marketing to build your investment fund?

No. It's just one method.

However, you're probably already doing network marketing (recommending and promoting what you like) every day, <u>but you're just not getting paid for it</u>. It might be worthwhile checking out the possibilities. After all, we don't want to be working for free if we're trying to build our investment fund, right?

If you're not already familiar with network marketing, it won't be hard to locate someone who can explain it to you.

Where should I invest my money?

I'm not going to tell you where to invest your money. That's a personal decision. Some people are comfortable with real estate. Some people invest by buying automobiles wholesale and reselling them at retail.

Other people invest in mutual funds because they want someone else to worry about the safety and return on their money. And still others invest in individual stocks and bonds because that is their area of expertise.

So should you invest in tax lien certificates or cattle? It's up to you.

The more aggressive your investment portfolio, the greater the chance of an impressive gain or unimpressive loss. Everyone has his own tolerance for risk.

Just make sure to consider the safety of your investment fund. A low return that insures your capital makes it easier to sleep at night.

However, if your expertise is in a certain type of investment, go for it. You'll get a better return as an expert when your wits are pitted against amateurs. I have a friend who buys surplus valves, reconditions them, and resells them to the general market. His return on investment is over 200% because he understands, and is an expert, in his market.

So if you know the ins and outs of the local real estate market, invest there. If you know the ins and outs of stocks and bonds, invest there.

And as a side note, one of the best places to invest is in yourself. If you invested $300 or $600 in a class or training that helps you earn an extra $1,000 or $2,000 a year, this would be a higher rate of return than almost any investment imaginable.

Always make sure to invest in yourself . . . unless you think you would be a bad investment.

A really short course on becoming rich.

Spend less than your earn – invest the difference.

This is the only way you can accumulate the money for your investment fund. Your money can't work for you if you don't have any money to put to work.

Sure, it takes a bit of sacrifice to put away $100 a month, $200 a month, 10% of your salary, or whatever you decide is right for you. But by sacrificing a little bit every month, you'll have all the money you want for years and years and years.

It is said:

> " A penny saved is . . . not very much."

That's probably true. However,

> "Saving 65 cents a day in pocket change will add up to tens of thousands of dollars over time."

Consider this. It's almost impossible to become rich by spending more than you earn. Most people spend more than they earn. Most people aren't rich.

Use a part-time job or a part-time business to add more money to your investment account.

By adding this extra income, you'll cut years off your personal plan to wealth. Getting rich quicker is good, right?

Use people leverage to add more money to your investment account.

You can turbocharge your journey to wealth by employing other people in your part-time business or by taking advantage of network marketing.

Buy things that appreciate. Don't buy things that depreciate.

Stocks, mutual funds, and real estate appreciate over time. That means your money is working for you. Stereos, fancy clothes, automobiles, and big screen televisions depreciate over time. That means you are going backwards – that you are losing money. That's not the way to get rich.

Own your own home.

Renters and homeowners both make payments every month. You won't get rich collecting rent receipts. You get rich by owning real estate.

Get a good tax accountant.

You want to minimize your taxes so that you'll have more money working for you in your investment account. Your tax accountant can show you ways to reduce, defer or eliminate taxes on your investments. You can reduce the effects of taxes on your extra income by investing through IRAs, Keogh plans, 401s and other tax-favorable investment vehicles.

If you are really worried about paying taxes on the extra money you are earning, simply work a few extra hours for the taxes or arrange to have extra taxes taken out of your regular paycheck.

Avoid debt.

Some types of debt are good. An example would be the mortgage on your home (assuming you've bought a home within your means). This is debt on an appreciating asset.

Most debts are bad because you are paying interest on that debt. Paying interest is having your money work against you. It is robbing your investment fund of valuable capital that could be used to work for you.

Worst of all is paying interest on a depreciating asset such as an automobile or stereo. Not only are you losing money by paying interest, but the item you are paying for is also losing value at the same time. That is what's called a "double whammy."

If you have a lot of debt siphoning away your salary, maybe the first place for you to invest your investment money is in reducing your debt. This will ultimately free up more money in your monthly budget that you can put into your investment program.

Start young – or as young as you can.

That means start now. Let time work for you, not against you. The longer your investment fund grows, the more money you'll have. Even if you invest very conservatively, time and the magic of compound interest will serve you well.

Don't be someone who says,

> "Oh, I wish I started ten years ago. Look where I would be today."

> "I should have invested in McDonald's and Chrysler stock back in 1972."

The past is past. You can't redesign your past. However, you can design your future.

So start designing your future today. Ten years from now will arrive whether you start saving and investing or not. The choice of what you'll say ten years from now depends on what you do today.

Protect your investment fund by reducing risk.

What good is it to save your money, only to lose it later on a speculative risk? It's better to have a lower return and all of your investment fund than a higher return and sleepless nights worrying about your money.

Certainly all investments have some risk. You'll want to keep your risks to a minimum while looking out for good returns.

You can invest your extra money monthly in a mutual fund, in real estate, to reduce your personal mortgage, or even in your own part-time or full-time business. Your investment risks decrease with knowledge.

Have patience.

Your investment fund won't grow rapidly overnight. Consistent investing will give your good returns in the long term. For example, when is the best time to invest in stocks?

The obvious answer is to invest at the beginning of a long bull market (rising prices). Since no one can accurately tell the future, the best time to start investing for most of us is right now. Obviously stock prices go down also. But a stock portfolio that goes down in price is worth much more than never investing or saving a cent.

Investors who have become rich in stocks have invested over a long period of time. That includes up markets and down markets.

Handle your finances like an adult.

How do four-year-olds handle money? Do four-year-olds use their allowance wisely — or do they spend it quickly on something they want? Usually they insist on spending their allowance the same day they receive it. Saving or creating an investment fund is the furthest thing from their mind.

If you handle your money like a four-year-old, you'll have the savings account of a four-year-old.

Don't worry about inflation.

Inflation will occur whether you save money or not. So why not save money? You'll like inflation a lot better when you have a large savings account.

Can't seem to find any money to start your investment program?

Try this. Now I'm not asking you to budget. I'm only going to ask you to keep track of where your money goes for 30 days. Here is what you do.

Take a blank register from your checkbook. Simply record every expense, every dollar you spend for one entire month. Write down when you buy a pack of gum, a pack of cigarettes, a soda, when you pay the VISA bill, when you buy that sandwich or movie ticket.

At the end of the month, review your register. Look at all the miscellaneous expenditures you made that could have been turned into investment dollars.

Will you do this? Only if you are serious about becoming rich.

I've seen people who earn $10,000 make regular contributions to their investment fund. I've also seen people earning $100,000 a year spend $110,000 a year and go bankrupt.

Saving money has nothing to do with how much money you make. It has everything to do with personal commitment.

And now it's up to you.

Now that you know the rules, your personal wealth is not dependent on chance. You can make the choice to be rich, to retire wealthy, and to have the time of your life!

Multiple copies of this book make perfect gifts that can change people's lives. If you need additional books, they can be purchased from:

KAAS Publishing
P.O. Box 890084
Houston, TX 77289
(281) 280-9800

www.FortuneNow.com

Want to know more?

This book was given to you as a gift by:

Are you serious about creating wealth? If so, contact the person above for your free copy of —

"22 More Tips To Help You Become Wealthy Fast"